JESUS FOR THE LAYMAN

ENCOUNTERING THE SON OF GOD

NEIL CULLAN McKINLAY

The question: 'Can you convince the reader Jesus is the Son of God?' Neil Cullan McKinlay picks up the gauntlet thrown down by a friend seeking the definitive answer to a question which has tested theologians for centuries. One man claimed to be 'the way, the truth, and the life'. He was nailed to a cross and cried out in dying despair: 'My God, My God, why have You forsaken Me?' Make no mistake: To understand precisely what happened here is to accept responsibility for your part in this. With this book, you will face a choice. Be careful what you wish for. The author - The answer: Neil Cullan McKinlay, is a Scots-Canadian who lives in Australia, where he is a chaplain in the Australian Defence Force. He is the author of 28 books, produced with his trademark touch of reducing elusive complexities to accessible simplicities. His path to Christ took him from his native Scotland to the harsh winters of Manitoba where he was given a book as a gift, the Bible. It was to be the gift of life. His ministry is characterised by the shipyard wit of his Scottish inheritance, and the robust thought conferred by the Reformation. Without ostentation and with Calvinist clarity, his work persists in turning everything to the service of Christ; yet he claims no credit for it.

'Can you convince the reader Jesus is the Son of God?' he is asked. His answer is simple: 'Let me be up front. I don't believe that I am able to do so. Only God can do that. However, God uses means to convince people of things.'

This book is such an instrument.

Published by WEEMAC Publishing

First printing: June 2019

A CIP catalogue for this title is available from the British Library.

ISBN: 978-1-908898-83-8

4

I dedicate this book to Billy Scobie,
a.k.a. Alexander Tait,
author of Whisky in the Jar,
The Cup,
Mightier Than the Sword,
Upon This Rock,
Song of the River,
a great writer and a long-time friend and encourager.

Buddha never claimed to be God. Moses never claimed to be Jehovah. Mohammed never claimed to be Allah. Yet Jesus Christ claimed to be the true and living God. Buddha simply said, "I am a teacher in search of the truth." Jesus said, "I am the Truth." Confucius said, "I never claimed to be holy." Jesus said, "Who convicts me of sin?" Mohammed said, "Unless God throws his cloak of mercy over me, I have no hope." Jesus said, "Unless you believe in Me, you will die in your sins."
– Unknown

Scripture Versions used:
King James' Version (KJV)
New King James Version (NKJV)
New International Version (NIV)
The New Living Translation (NLT)

Other books by Neil Cullan McKinlay
(Hardcover):
FROM MASON TO MINISTER: Through the Lattice
(Paperback):
THE SONG OF CREATION & Other Contemplations
JEFFERSON'S TEARS
(E-books):
THE NEXUS: The True Nature of Nature
ARE ALL WHO DIE IN INFANCY SAVED?
DEMYSTIFYING THE GOSPEL
HOLDING FAST OUR CONFESSION
WESTMINSTER SHORTER CATECHISM ELABORATED
ON THE LORD'S TABLE
ON THE CHURCH
PAVING PARADISE
COVENANT SIMPLIFIED
THE WORKS OF THE FLESH *VERSUS* THE FRUIT OF THE SPIRIT
THE BLEST, THE REST, & THE BEST
MORAL INJURY: Towards a Theology
I BELIEVE! The Apostles' Creed
ABRAHAM: Father of the Faithful
THE SONG OF CREATION & Other Contemplations
UNDER GOD'S RAINBOW & Other Contemplations
DISEMBARK THE ARK & Other Contemplations
CURTAIN CALL & Other Contemplations
BEAUTY & Other Contemplations
MYTHS & MYSTERIES & Other Contemplations
A STICK IN TIME (Novel)
JEFFERSON'S TEARS
FROM MASON TO MINISTER: Through the Lattice
THISTLES & GUM TREES (Short Stories)
MASONIC MUSINGS
SOCIALISM: My Part in its Downfall

Preface

This short book is the result of an idea suggested to me by an old friend, that I should write a book about Jesus, but make it for the layman. My friend had a specific goal in mind: "Try to convince the reader why he should believe that Jesus is the Son of God." That is the approach I've taken in the following. I am trying to convince you (the reader) that you should believe that Jesus is who the Bible says He is, i.e., the Son of God.

Let me be up front. I don't believe that I am able to convince you that Jesus is the Son of God. Only God can do that. However, God uses means to convince people of things. He uses His written Word and He is pleased at times to use those who expound that written Word. In other words, there are people (like me for example) who become convinced of Jesus's identity simply through reading the Bible. But ordinarily it's through someone explaining to you what the Bible has to say about Jesus. I'll use the story about Philip the Evangelist and the Ethiopian eunuch to illustrate this:

> This man had gone to Jerusalem to worship, and on his way home was sitting in his chariot reading the Book of Isaiah the prophet. The Spirit told Philip, 'Go to that chariot and stay near it.' Then Philip ran up to the chariot and heard the man reading Isaiah the prophet. 'Do you understand what you are reading?' Philip asked. 'How can I,' he said, 'unless someone explains it to me?' So he invited Philip to come up and sit with him. This is the passage of Scripture the eunuch was reading: 'He was led like a sheep to the slaughter, and as a lamb before its shearer is silent, so he did not open his mouth. In his humiliation he

was deprived of justice. Who can speak of his descendants? For his life was taken from the earth.' The eunuch asked Philip, 'Tell me please, who is the prophet talking about, himself or someone else?' Then Philip began with that very passage of Scripture and told him the good news about Jesus.

Dear reader, will you invite me to, as it were, come up and sit with you in your chariot and, as we read some passages of Scripture together, allow me to attempt to explain to you how they testify that Jesus is the Son of God? Will you permit me, as the Ethiopian eunuch did Philip, to tell you the good news about Jesus? The Ethiopian went on to be baptised by Philip, obviously being convinced of the Good News about Jesus.

There are books aplenty that are filled with theological technicalities about Jesus. This is not one of them. As the title says, this book is about Jesus For the Layman. I'll try to engage you with interesting examples and illustrations from everyday life, including my own personal anecdotes. However, the bottom line of everything that follows is that my main desire and prayer for you the reader is that you will have an actual and personal encounter with Jesus Christ. That He will be pleased to meet with you and make an impact on you during our interaction through what I have written even in this wee book.

CONTENTS

Introduction

We live in an age in which the name Jesus is casually used as a swear word – even in polite company! Many laymen (or should I say "laypersons"?) have no idea or don't care who Jesus is. There has been a seismic shift, as they say, in society. No longer can it be assumed even in churches that people really know who Jesus is, let alone actually know Him personally.

I didn't grow up with a church background. Most of my formative years were spent in a nice wee village on the southern end of Loch Lomond just north of Glasgow.[1] Church for me consisted of Christmas Day and Easter services. The focus of these of course revolved around the birth, death and resurrection of Jesus. We would sing children's hymns like Away in a Manger and the more adult What a Friend We Have in Jesus.

With his usual humour, Billy Connolly reminded us that as children we would sometimes get the words mixed-up and sing "A wean[2] in a manger..." The Lord's Prayer[3] became "Our Father which art in heaven, Harold be Thy name..." "The cross-eyed bear" etc. Has the simple message about Jesus also become garbled?

The Bible says that we are to have a childlike faith, not a childish one. But I fear that society has lost Jesus somewhere along the way, that we may have left Him behind. Like the men on the road to Emmaus we used to walk and talk with Jesus and He with us. Now we just seem

---

[1] One time when I was back in Scotland a friend gave me a copy of Jamie Stuart's A Glasgow Bible which is written in the Glasgow vernacular (i.e., Glaswegian).

[2] A wean like a bairn is a child.

[3] "Our Faither in heiven, hallowt be thy name..," – see The New Testament in Scots translated by William Laughton Lorimer.

to focus on our own selves. Even those steeped in theology can end up walking around simply with an idea of Jesus rather than with Him personally! This was brought home to me by my eldest brother one time at Glasgow Airport as he was farewelling me on my return from Scotland to Australia. Here's roughly what happened:

My wife, two brothers, a sister, and their partners, and a nephew and I were all sitting in a circle in bucket seats having a coffee before my wife and I were to take to the skies after spending a month with them in Scotland.

I'm usually nervous about flying (and/or roller-coaster rides!), so I welcomed the conversation I had with my eldest brother as a nice distraction. The dialogue went deep. I felt as if I should have been engaging with the others too, but my big brother had my almost undivided attention. He wanted to get the point across that theology and its propositions is not God, but only one of many pointers to God. In other words, we can become guilty of confusing a signpost for the actual destination, an analogy for the reality.

I asked my brother if the "Ceci n'est pas une pipe" (i.e., the famous "This is Not a Pipe") painting illustrated what he was driving at. (My brother is, among other things, an artist.) The point being that an actual pipe and a painting of a pipe are two different things. We discussed how God reveals Himself by way of analogy, i.e., through the things He has made and also what He has said in written revelation, the Bible.

We sipped on our coffees as airport announcements interrupted our verbal interaction. As the precious minutes ticked away, lest I missed his point, he put his hand on my arm and referred to the Bible passage where Jesus said to Martha after her brother Lazarus had died, "Your brother will rise again." Martha answered, "I know he will rise again in the resurrection at the last day." My brother said that Martha was thinking in terms of theology, i.e., propositional truth. She knew about the resurrection that will take place at the last day. This is what the Bible teaches.

However, Martha was missing the point, a major point. And, so that I would not miss it too, my big brother began yanking on my arm sharply while saying the words Jesus said to Martha, "I am the resurrection..." Jesus was saying that He is not a theological proposition, a painting of Himself, a signpost, a mere analogy. He was saying, I AM the resurrection!"

Wow! I felt as if I really met Jesus at Glasgow Airport.

It is my prayer that you will meet Jesus in the following and not just an idea of Him, but really meet Him!

Person or Picture?

What comes to mind whenever you think of Jesus? Some longhaired bearded guy all robes and sandals? Would it surprise you to learn that nowhere does the Bible tell us what Jesus looked like? Yet most movies and books picture Him as if He were a blue-eyed hippy left over from the 60s cultural revolution! The Bible says of Him, "He has no beauty or majesty to attract us to Him, nothing in His appearance that we should desire Him."[4] But Jesus is usually depicted as a handsome man in the movies.

One is left wondering where the contemporary picture of Jesus comes from, as most people see Him depicted in pictures. My own theory is that it is the imprint on The Shroud of Turin[5] that is the basis for the

---

[4] Isaiah 53:2b. (NIV)
[5] The Shroud of Turin is alleged by some to be a burial cloth that wrapped the crucified, dead and buried Jesus Christ. The linen cloth bears the image of a man.

contemporary picture of Jesus that springs to mind. (Dear reader please feel free to disagree with me on this, but for the record, I'm not convinced of the shroud's authenticity.[6]) I think the closest the Bible comes to describing how Jesus looked is found in the following: "His eyes will be darker than wine, His teeth whiter than milk."[7]

I don't know about you, but I suppose I would like Jesus to be tall, dark and handsome with movie-star looks. Why? Because isn't that the way a hero, the star of the Bible, is supposed to look? Well, maybe not. The Bible is full of paradoxes, "the last shall be first", "the meek shall inherit the earth", "you must lose your life to find it" etc. Jesus is the Bible's biggest paradox!

Let me repeat that verse: "He has no beauty or majesty to attract us to Him, nothing in His appearance that we should desire Him." This is not exactly the Hollywood version of a hero! I put it to you that if we are going to meet with and have an encounter with Jesus we shall need to make sure that we are able to recognise Him, lest we despise and reject Him out of hand as some imposter! Therefore, it probably is best if you do not have any picture

---

[6] The Shroud of Turin? My study of the Scriptures showed me that Jesus was not wrapped in a burial shroud, but was wrapped in strips of linen with a face cloth over His face. (See Mark 15:46; Luke 23:53.) Also, "Then they took the body of Jesus, and bound it in strips of linen with the spices, as the custom of the Jews is to bury." John 19:40 with "Then Simon Peter came, following him, and went into the tomb; and he saw the linen cloths lying there, and the handkerchief that had been around His head, not lying with the linen cloths, but folded together in a place by itself." John 20:6-7.
[7] Genesis 49:12.

of Jesus in mind.[8] Indeed, that would be why there is scant (if any) description in the Bible of how Jesus looks. I hope to say more on this a little later.

In the Braveheart movie, the Scottish army failed to recognize William Wallace when he showed up to lead them into battle. They were expecting a giant of a man, not someone of the relatively short stature of Mel Gibson! However, they couldn't fail to recognize him in his rousing pre-battle speech. He spoke to men's hearts, of things, deep things, things about freedom. Here's a wee sample:

> "Sons of Scotland! I am William Wallace."
> *Soldier: William Wallace is seven feet tall!*
> "Yes, I've heard. Kills men by the hundred! And if he were here, he'd consume the English with fireballs from his eyes, and bolts of lightning from his arse! I am William Wallace. And I see a whole army of my countrymen, here in defiance of tyranny. You've come to fight as free men. And free men you are. What will you do with that freedom? Will you fight? *Soldier 2: "Fight? Against that? No! We will run. And we will live."*

---

[8] My own personal reasoning in brief is as follows: I would suggest that pictures of Jesus and God (including the ones you and I may have in our minds) are in breach of the 2nd Commandment: "You shall not make for yourself an image in the form of anything in heaven above or on the earth beneath or in the waters below. You shall not bow down to them or worship them; for I, the LORD your God, am a jealous God, punishing the children for the sin of the parents to the third and fourth generation of those who hate me, [6] but showing love to a thousand generations of those who love me and keep my commandments." Exodus 20:4-6. Jesus is God the Son and we must not separate His humanity from His divinity. Sure, I've seen gazillions of pictures supposedly depicting Jesus. But that, to my mind, still does not make it right.

"Aye, fight and you may die. Run, and you'll live. At least a while. – And dying in your beds, many years from now, would you be willing to trade all the days from this day to that, for one chance, just one chance, to come back here and tell our enemies, that they may take our lives, but they'll never take our freedom!"

Wallace (in the movie) was not what the Scottish troops had pictured in their minds, i.e., some spectacular giant of a man. However, though "a picture is worth a thousand words" the picture is not the reality. (Google the "This is not a Pipe" painting.) It ever remains a picture. At best it is a flawed depiction of reality. And so it is with Jesus. Like the Scottish troops' picture of William Wallace before they had actually encountered him, so our picture of Jesus may be a thousand miles away from the reality. But the focus is not upon what He looks like, but rather on the fact that when He speaks to you, He will speak directly to your heart, of things, deep things, things of freedom.

Do not settle for a mere picture of Jesus. Insist on the reality!

The Word of God

I remember someone saying to me that they had tried to read the Bible but gave up because they didn't like blood and gore! Like the Braveheart movie the Bible contains lots of graphic scenes. Yes, there is blood, gore and swords buried up to the hilt in human flesh! To be sure there are lots of tender moments too in both. However, unlike the Braveheart movie, instead of pictures, the Bible uses only words to tell its story. The words of the Bible are able to penetrate us even to our innermost being. "For the word of God is alive and active. Sharper than any double-edged sword, it penetrates even to dividing soul and spirit, joints and marrow; it judges the thoughts and attitudes of the heart." Hebrews 4:12.

I was lamenting the fact that nowadays movies feel the need to show the blood and gore bits even in slow-motion without leaving much to the imagination. I think things started going downhill after the 1974 Texas Chainsaw Massacre movie which was remade in 2003. I've never actually seen either of these! However, the point I wish to make is an important one for what we're looking at. Like the old Alfred Hitchcock movies, apparently the 1974 Texas Chainsaw massacre movie leaves most of the gore to the imagination. In other words, you get the picture! In some ways this can be more confronting and indeed more frightening than seeing fake blood. It's the difference between seeing a mere picture of something, even something gory, and that of understanding and experiencing the reality! You don't just see it, you feel it! The point being therefore, when you read the Bible about Jesus, don't forget that He uses His Word as a mind-probe, "it judges the thoughts and attitudes of the heart." Here Jesus is seen with the mind's-eye, not with the physical eye. Your spirit encounters and feels it, not your body.

The Bible is sometimes referred to as the Sword of the Spirit. It is what Jesus used when He was being tempted in the wilderness by that evil spirit-being, i.e., Satan, a.k.a. the tempter. For example, "The tempter came to Him and said, 'If you are the Son of God, tell these stones to become bread.' Jesus answered, 'It is written: 'Man shall not live on bread alone, but on every word that comes from the mouth of God.'" Jesus just quoted relevant verses of Scripture to Satan and eventually Satan left Him to fight another day. But the point (pun intended!) is that the Word of God is sharper than any double-edged sword (including the likes of Wallace's claymore!) Jesus deftly wields the Sword of the Spirit, i.e., the Word of God to fight spiritual battles against spiritual forces.

The Bible itself claims to be written by God using men. And, call it circular reasoning if you wish, but Jesus believed that the Bible we have today was written by God. From Moses to the Apostle John all the Bible authors were moved by the Spirit of God, each using his own ordinary way of writing, to write down what God wanted them to write down, every jot and tittle of it. There are sixty-six Books of the Bible written over a period of some fourteen hundred years by over forty authors. The Bible was completed not too many years after Jesus died and was resurrected.

It is the Bible itself that must convince you that it is the written Word of God. Or better, it is the Spirit of Christ working with the Word of God that must convince you that it is God's Word. This is what we mean by Jesus deftly wielding the Sword of the Spirit. He uses it to stab certain people in the heart with His Word. But, and as we have already mentioned that the Bible is full of paradoxes, rather than killing you, getting stabbed in the heart by the Sword of the Spirit actually brings you back to life! It means that you have become alive spiritually, which in turn means that, unlike before, you are now ready to listen to God as He speaks (to you) with His Word!

Speaking of chainsaws, there was a funny story about a man who took his chainsaw back to the hardware store complaining that it wouldn't cut the amount of wood in the time the advertisement said it would. The store-man pulled the cord and started up the chainsaw. The complaining customer with a startled look on his face yelled, "What's that noise?" The Bible is like that for some people. It's never been fired-up! It collects dust. The Book is used as a good luck charm and nothing more. However, the Word of God has to be activated by the Spirit of Christ, i.e. the Holy Spirit working with the Word in your heart before you will hear it. Otherwise it will remain as silent as that chainsaw in the hands of that complaining customer. A word to the wise, always remember that: "The word of God is alive and active."

In the Bible Jesus is known as the Word. See if you can hear this: "In the beginning was the Word, and the Word was with God, and the Word was God. He was with God in the beginning. Through Him all things were made; without Him nothing was made that has been made … The Word became flesh and made His dwelling among us." John 1:1-3 & 14a.

The Word of God says that Jesus is the Word of God who in the beginning was with God and was God. The Bible speaks of Christ Jesus from cover to cover. As Jesus said of the Scriptures to some men, "You study the Scriptures diligently because you think that in them you have eternal life. These are the very Scriptures that testify about Me." John 5:39.

Are you ready and willing to hear what the Scriptures have to say about Jesus?

Meeting Jesus

Before we go about meeting Jesus, by which we mean encountering Jesus, let me paint in a bit more background scenery. As I mentioned above, growing up and attending school in the Vale of Leven on the West Coast of Scotland during the 1960s meant that I was taken to church with the other pupils at Christmas and Easter. For perhaps obvious reasons, as a child ordinarily I preferred the Christmas services over the Easter ones. The former being about the birth of Jesus and the latter about His death and subsequent resurrection. I loved the baby Jesus – mangers, wise men and shepherds. And, hey, it was Christmas and that meant Christmas presents! Easter was all about rolling painted boiled eggs down hills to me. The man on the cross remained a mystery. What was he doing on that cross? Taking away sins or something. I don't think sins or transgressions or whatever they were ever was explained to us. Then Jesus came alive again. And went to heaven. Whoopee! Let's have some chocolate Easter eggs instead of boiled ones (with bits of broken eggshell).

Though His birth and death are no less worthy of study, it's at the cross that we must meet Jesus if we are to understand who He is and what it is He has done.

Now, dear reader I apologize to you and hope you can forgive me, but I've already primed you up for a discussion about Jesus that some have called "Butcher Shop Theology", you know, where Christians talk about being saved by the blood of Jesus and all that. By the disparaging term "Butcher Shop Theology" they mean that Christians enter into too much blood and gore by talking about Christ's cross. But Christ without the cross is like an ocean without water. Crossless Christianity is meaningless. No cross and the Bible is rendered meaningless.

A man asked me, a marriage celebrant, to marry him and his partner. I said, "but you're an Atheist! Why would you want a Christian preacher for a celebrant?" After some discussion I put this to him, "Let me see, you like Christianity without Christ?" "Yes!" he responded. Well, just as a crossless Christ is meaningless, so is Christianity without Christ, the real Christ!

The Bible says, "Jesus Christ is the same yesterday and today and forever" Hebrews 13:8. We don't get to change Him or to mould Him into the way we would like Him to be. We don't get to meet with a caricature of Jesus, a Jesus who wouldn't hurt a fly, a Jesus who never shed His blood on a cross. We don't change Jesus. Jesus changes us!

But first you have to meet Him, encounter Him by drawing near to Him. For Scripture says, "Come near to God and He will come near to you" James 4:8. But keep the following in mind. Jesus says, "No one can come to Me unless the Father who sent Me draws them, and I will raise them up at the last day" John 6:44. Paradox? We are to draw near to God but we won't unless the Father draws us? Wait a minute, I hear you say. Is it God or is it Jesus I'm supposed to be drawing near to? Let me put it to you, to draw near to God is to draw near to Jesus, because God and Jesus are the same! Scriptures says, "For there is one God and one mediator between God and mankind, the man Christ Jesus" 1 Timothy 2:5a. And Jesus says, "I am the way and the truth and the life. No one comes to the Father except through Me." John 14:6.

Yes, that's a lot to be getting on with! But the bottom line is that to meet with Jesus is to meet with God. And, regardless of the blood and gore, the best place to meet with Jesus is at His cross.

Are you ready for some more Bible paradoxes? The Father poured out His anger on His Son as He hung nailed to wooden cross! Why was God the Father angry with God the Son? He wasn't! Don't miss it. God was not angry with Jesus Christ His only begotten Son. God was angry with us. He was angry with you and He was angry with me! What did I do, what did you do, what did we do to make God angry with us that He needed to pour out His wrath upon His Son to take away our sins? There's that mysterious word again, "sins."

We've already noted that "Jesus Christ is the same yesterday and today and forever." He was sinless yesterday,

He was sinless today, and He is sinless forever. It was our sins, our iniquities that God was dealing with when Christ was hanging on the cross.

I know the following is lengthy, but even though it was written five hundred years before the event of the cross, it is worth reading. I've underlined the bits that speak of Jesus dying for our sins and I will give a little commentary:

> "Who has believed our message and to whom has the arm of the Lord been revealed? He grew up before Him like a tender shoot, and like a root out of dry ground. He had no beauty or majesty to attract us to Him, nothing in His appearance that we should desire Him. He was despised and rejected by mankind, a man of suffering, and familiar with pain. Like one from whom people hide their faces He was despised, and we held Him in low esteem. Surely He took up our pain and bore our suffering, yet we considered Him punished by God, stricken by Him, and afflicted."

Why did Jesus go all the way to the cross to receive the wrath of God?

> "But He was pierced for our transgressions, He was crushed for our iniquities; the punishment that brought us peace was on Him, and by His wounds we are healed."

Why did Jesus need to go to the cross in the first place?

> "We all, like sheep, have gone astray, each of us has turned to our own way; and the Lord has laid on Him

the iniquity of us all. He was oppressed and afflicted, yet He did not open His mouth; He was led like a lamb to the slaughter, and as a sheep before its shearers is silent, so He did not open His mouth. By oppression and judgment He was taken away. Yet who of His generation protested? For He was cut off from the land of the living; for the transgression of my people He was punished. He was assigned a grave with the wicked, and with the rich in His death, though He had done no violence, nor was any deceit in his mouth."

And then speaking of the resurrection of Jesus Christ,

"Yet it was the Lord's will to crush Him and cause Him to suffer, and though the Lord makes His life an offering for sin, He will see His offspring and prolong His days, and the will of the Lord will prosper in His hand. After He has suffered, He will see the light of life and be satisfied; by His knowledge My righteous servant will justify many, and He will bear their iniquities. Therefore I will give Him a portion among the great, and He will divide the spoils with the strong, because He poured out His life unto death, and was numbered with the transgressors. For He bore the sin of many, and made intercession for the transgressors." Isaiah 53:1-12.

All the bloody animal sacrifices in the Old Testament Scriptures pointed to Him of whom John the Baptist said, "Look, the Lamb of God, who takes away the sin of the world!" John 1:29. "But if we walk in the light, as He is in the light, we have fellowship with one another, and the blood of Jesus, His Son, purifies us from all sin." 1 John 1:7. O, and what is sin? "Everyone who sins breaks the law; in fact, sin is lawlessness" 1 John 3:4. Thus sin is the transgressing or breaking of God's Law, summarised in His Ten Commandments (i.e., the Decalogue) either in thought or in word or in deed.

Jesus had no sin of His own, but He took upon Himself the sins of all who believe in Him so that the Father's justice could be paid and His righteous anger toward sin could be assuaged. "Therefore, there is now no condemnation for those who are in Christ Jesus' Romans 8:1. If you are a believer in Jesus Christ your sins have been covered by His shed blood. God does not look at you as a sinner. He looks at Jesus as your Saviour. In other words, Jesus represents you before God. You have been declared in God's court of law as "righteous" because of what Jesus did. It's a legal transaction: Your sins were given to Jesus on the cross and His righteousness was given to you. You are now sinless. Call it "Butcher Shop Theology" if you want! But it is the Gospel, the Good News of Jesus Christ about Jesus Christ.

If you have met with Christ at His cross and have witnessed Him hanging there, then here's the view from His side of things as He hung on that tree, written a thousand years before He died. Read it slowly, taking it in, feeling His pain on that cross:

> "But I am a worm and not a man, scorned by everyone, despised by the people. All who see Me mock Me; they hurl insults, shaking their heads. "He trusts in the Lord," they say, "let the Lord rescue Him. Let Him deliver Him, since He delights in Him." Yet you brought Me out of the womb; you made Me trust in You, even at my mother's breast. From birth

I was cast on You; from My mother's womb You have been My God. Do not be far from Me, for trouble is near and there is no one to help. Many bulls surround Me, strong bulls of Bashan encircle Me. Roaring lions that tear their prey open their mouths wide against Me. I am poured out like water, and all My bones are out of joint. My heart has turned to wax; it has melted within Me. My mouth is dried up like a potsherd, and My tongue sticks to the roof of My mouth; you lay Me in the dust of death. Dogs surround Me, a pack of villains encircles Me; they pierce My hands and My feet. All My bones are on display, people stare and gloat over Me. They divide My clothes among them and cast lots for My garment. But you, Lord, do not be far from Me. You are My strength; come quickly to help Me. Deliver Me from the sword, My precious life from the power of the dogs. Rescue Me from the mouth of the lions; save Me from the horns of the wild oxen." Psalm 22:6-21.

When Jesus was born, a man called Simeon spoke to Jesus' mother, Mary. "And Simeon blessed them and said to Mary His mother, "Behold, this *Child* is appointed for the fall and rise of many in Israel, and for a sign to be opposed—and a sword will pierce even your own soul—to the end that thoughts from many hearts may be revealed." Luke 2:34-35.

Has the Sword of the Spirit pierced your heart, especially as you met with Jesus at His cross?

The Son of God

Lots of people who saw Jesus when He walked on this earth did not believe that He was who He said He was, i.e., the Son of God. Obviously, these people had a different picture of Jesus in mind to that revealed in Scripture.

There was, however, a Roman soldier who no doubt was familiar with the blood and gore of war and even the torture of Jesus, who believed that Jesus was the Son of God. "And when the centurion, who stood there in front of Jesus, saw how He died, he said, 'Surely this Man was the Son of God!'" Mark 15:39.

It would be too simple if, when the Bible refers to Jesus as the Son of God and the Son of Man, that the former referred only to His divinity (as in being God) and the latter referred only to His being a human. For we need to keep in mind that being called the Son of God was not unique to Jesus. For example, the Bible refers to Adam as the Son of God.[9] However, note that Adam was directly created by God using the dust of the earth as the substance for his humanity,[10] and Jesus, the last Adam, the second Man,[11] was also created by God using Mary as the substance for His humanity.[12] But the point here is that the centurion, unlike those who mocked Jesus on the cross, believed that Jesus actually was the Son of God. Likewise, we need to make sure that we are believing in the right Jesus Christ and not some imposter or figment of our imagination.

This centurion had heard Jesus on the cross utter these words, "My God, My God, why have You forsaken Me?" Mark 15:34. These words are taken from the first

---

[9] Luke 3:38.
[10] Genesis 2:7; 1 Corinthians 15:47-48.
[11] 1 Corinthians 15:45;47.
[12] Luke 1:31;35.

verse of Psalm 22, (the Psalm we quoted above). The words express the anguish of Hellish torment that Christ was experiencing at that time in His human body and soul. Jesus was less concerned about being forsaken by family and friends than by being forsaken by God! We need to put on the brakes a wee bit here. Lest we get into trouble with those who are sticklers for making sure that we have the correct Jesus, i.e., the Jesus of the Bible. So let us progress slowly.

Why would Jesus mention being forsaken by God at this point as He hung on the cross? Well, keep in mind that there was a great exchange taking place on that cross. The New Living Translation of the Bible does well explaining what was happening here where it says, "For God made Christ, who never sinned, to be the offering for our sin, so that we could be made right with God through Christ." Did you get that? The great exchange is that when God sacrificed His Son Jesus He was at the same time reconciling Himself to us and us to Him. Yes, He was also reconciling us to Him. Jesus, the perfect Man, was the only thing that could represent us. Bulls, sheep and goats could never substitute for human beings. And, because Jesus is also God as well as human His human sacrifice is of infinite worth.

Jesus is God and Man in one divine Person forever. He is not two persons, but one person with two distinct natures, the divine and the human. This is where we need to get ready to start talking about God being triune in nature, i.e., Father and Son and Holy Spirit, three Persons, but one God. The question then becomes: Can any Person in the Godhead forsake any of the Other Persons? Can the Father *really* forsake the Son who said, "My God. My God why have You forsaken Me"?

We must realize that God cannot look upon sin, even my sin and your sin. Scripture says of God, "Your eyes are too pure to look on evil; You cannot tolerate wrongdoing.' Habakkuk 1:13a. Jesus had become a sin-offering to God on the cross. God had imputed or transferred our sins to Jesus on the cross. Then He poured out His wrath, i.e., hellfire, on His Son consuming all of our sins. It was this wrath of God that killed Jesus as it was poured out upon Him (instead of us).

Do you understand now why Jesus might be feeling forsaken in His human spirit? A few lines from a well-known hymn spell it out for us. But before we go there, let me say that I really appreciate the words attached to this hymn and the other Scottish- or Celtic-sounding tunes and hymns the following hymnist has written. The words and tunes speak to the Celt in me:

How deep the Father's love for us
How vast beyond all measure
That He should give His only Son
To make a wretch His treasure
How great the pain of searing loss
The Father turns His face away
As wounds which mar the Chosen One
Bring many sons to glory
Behold the man upon a cross
My sin upon His shoulders
Ashamed, I hear my mocking voice
Call out among the scoffers
It was my sin that held Him there
Until it was accomplished
His dying breath has brought me life
I know that it is finished.[13]

---

[13] How Deep the Father's Love For Us, Stuart Townend: https://youtu.be/pmzudzkGS-Q

If you were to search the Internet you would discover that the author of this hymn has gotten himself into trouble with other Christians for writing those lines, "How great the pain of searing loss, The Father turns His face away." We can't have the Father forsaking the Son! That just won't do! It might suggest the Jesus is not God the middle Person in the Trinity but merely a human being like the rest of us!

Please don't balk at the fact that Christians take each other to task over such things. Why? Because this is a good thing! For it helps us to keep the Jesus who is revealed in the Bible before our eyes and not some figment of our own or another's imagination. You don't ever want to end up following the wrong Jesus!

So then, what's wrong with Jesus feeling forsaken even though technically He wasn't being forsaken by God? Have you ever *felt* forsaken? Well, apparently so has Jesus! Let's tease this out a little more.

As God accounted our sins to Jesus as He hung there on the cross, Jesus could feel in His humanity that there was now, for the first time, a barrier between Him and God! He had our sin on His shoulders! That's why He cried out, "My God, My God, why have You forsaken Me?" It shows us that He really did have our sins as He represented us. This was the wrath of God being poured out on His Son. It was total torment and absolute agony of soul for Jesus Christ – an excruciating feeling of forsakenness, abandonment. Hell is to be forsaken by God for *eternity*. And because Jesus is God and Man in one Divine Person forever, His suffering went out into all eternity and has eternal consequences – everlasting life for all who believe in Him.

Now, we really do need to be careful here. God the Father never for an instant stopped loving God the Son. God cannot deny Himself. Therefore, what Jesus was experiencing was a *feeling* of forsakenness *only* in His *human* nature. As God, as it were, turned His face away from Him Jesus experienced agony of soul. Thus, He experienced Hell on the cross. And isn't Hell utter darkness? Forsakenness? God holocausted our sin as He slew His Son, the sacrificial Lamb, by hanging Him upon the cursed tree, i.e., the cross. God cannot die. Therefore, it was in regard to His human nature, not His divine nature, that Jesus felt forsaken and subsequently died.

I hope that, like the centurion, *you* really do believe that Jesus is the Son of God.

God the Word

We need to dive a little deeper here. Jesus is the Son of God. But is He God the Son? After He was resurrected and before He had ascended back to the Father Jesus said these words to His disciples, "Go ye therefore, and teach all nations, baptizing them in the name of the Father, and of the Son, and of the Holy Ghost." The term "Holy Ghost" is simply another way of saying "Holy Spirit." We speak of the Father as being the first Person in the Godhead (or "Trinity"[14]), the Son as the second Person, and the Spirit being the third Person. The Son, the second or middle Person in the Trinity is also called the Word.

> "In the beginning was the Word, and the Word was with God, and the Word was God. He was in the beginning with God. All things were made through Him, and without Him nothing was made that was

---

[14] The word Trinity is not found in the Bible, but we use it to describe the Godhead.

made... And the Word became flesh and dwelt among us." John 1:1-3;14.

So we see then that it was not the Father or the Spirit who became a human being. It was only the Son or Word who became a human being. He was like us in every way apart from our sin. However, keep in mind that the Word never stopped being God. The eternal Son of God simply clothed Himself in flesh, as in body, soul and spirit. When Jesus was conceived by the Holy Spirit in the womb of Mary,[15] who was a virgin at the time, it was the Creator entering His creation as a human being.

The humanity of Jesus, like any other human being, began at the very moment of His conception. That is when the Word became flesh. However, He never stopped being the eternal Word of God. God the Son is the eternal Son of God the Father from all eternity. But Jesus only began to exist in time at the precise moment of His conception in Mary's womb. Jesus, therefore, is God and Man in one Divine Person forever. In other words, because Jesus has two natures, the divine and the human, God and Man meet and were forever reconciled in Him when God resurrected Him from the dead. Jesus can never ever die again!

The Good News, for that is what "Gospel" means, is about the triune God reconciling us to Himself and Himself to us by, in and through His Son Jesus Christ. We love the simplicity of the Gospel whereby Jesus Christ is the Saviour of sinners – that whosoever believes in Him shall not perish but have everlasting life (John 3:16). But we also love the profundity of the Gospel – that it's on account of Jesus being a Divine Person that His salvation is of infinite worth and His work on earth goes out into eternity.

---

[15] Luke 1:34-35.

Every Christmas when we sing Christmas carols Charles Wesley the hymnist reminds us that he got it right:

> Hark the herald angels sing
> Glory to the newborn King!
> Peace on earth and mercy mild
> God and sinners reconciled
> Joyful, all ye nations rise
> Join the triumph of the skies
> With the angelic host proclaim:
> Christ is born in Bethlehem
> Hark! The herald angels sing
> Glory to the newborn King!
> Christ by highest heav'n adored
> Christ the everlasting Lord
> Late in time behold Him come
> Offspring of a Virgin's womb
> Veiled in flesh the Godhead see
> Hail the incarnate Deity
> Pleased as man with man to dwell
> Jesus, our Emmanuel
> Hark! The herald angels sing
> Glory to the newborn King!

Growing up in Balloch, Loch Lomond had its benefits. As youths we got to swim in Loch Lomond every "summer." Yes, the water could be quite frigid at times! Not quite as exotic as say pearl diving, we used to dive off Balloch Pier whenever the Maid of the Loch paddle steamer that docked there was out on one of its excursions. Instead of pearl containing clams we used to retrieve plates and glasses that had been thrown overboard from the boat.

Speaking of pearls, Jesus says, "Do not give what is holy to the dogs; nor cast your pearls before swine, lest they trample them under their feet, and turn and tear you in pieces." Matthew 7:6. Casting pearls before swine can refer to things like explaining the deeper things of God to those who won't appreciate them. But, if you've read this far it can be assumed that you are interested in the deeper things of God. So let's dive deeper, not for old dinner plates, but for precious pearls.

God made man in His own image and likeness. But this image and likeness of God is not exhaustive. Unlike man who is finite, God is infinite. Therefore, God is not the image and likeness of man – which would be to confuse or mix our created human nature with His eternally uncreated and unchanging Divine nature. God does not absorb anything in or of nature. Nor does creation absorb anything in or of God. God transcends matter.

The eternal Second Person of the Trinity, the Word, became flesh in time but continued unchanged as God. Christ's incarnation, resurrection, and ascension prove that the divine and human are and will remain two distinct natures forever. Christ's human nature with its passions (pain, anguish of soul, hunger, thirst etc.), are forever distinct from His Divine nature. Yet God knows these passions in the same way He knows good and evil (Genesis 3:22), but experiences none of these because He is without passions in and of Himself.

Jesus Christ is the same, yesterday, today, and forever.[16] He is a Divine Person. Neither His divine nor human nature changed at His crucifixion. Jesus did not become a sinner on the cross. He became a sin-offering, and as such, received God's out poured fiery wrath. But Jesus suffered only in His human nature which remained distinct from His divine nature.

---

[16] Hebrew 13:8.

Was God pleased, or angry with Christ on the cross? One might as well ask whether Christ was angry or pleased with Himself on the cross? That is the question! Was there a conflict between His two natures? Was His Divine nature angry at His human nature – as God poured out His anger upon Him as He bore our sins? And was His human nature angry at His divine nature for the suffering caused? All paradoxes between the Divine and human (even God and creation) are resolved by keeping the two natures of Christ distinct. Confuse them and both the nature of God and man begin to change: Man becomes God and God becomes man. But either way both disappear like the metaphorical snake that swallowed its own tail!

In Christ God (the Word) and man are one in unity but not in substance. The properties of both natures may be ascribed to the One Person, i.e., Jesus Christ. But the nature of His Divinity must not be ascribed to the nature of His humanity, nor vice versa. Thus the Man Jesus Christ's anger (overturning tables etc.) may very well be an expression of what is understood to be God's anger.

However, because all revelation of God is not exhaustive and is only analogous, one sees in the Man Christ Jesus' anger more a revelation of God's Holy nature than of any supposed human passion of anger. Christ's anger is revelation of God's holiness, not God's anger. To say that God was both pleased and angry at the same time when Christ hung on the cross is to speak metaphorically of the holiness and righteousness of God. For God revealed who and what He is at the cross. But we must not confuse God's anger or His pleasure with human passions. The nature of God who made the heavens, the earth, and all that are in them was not changed by His creation nor by Christ's cross.

All creation is revelation of who and what God is: even Hell itself! All creation therefore, though solid and real, is a metaphor of God. Christ is the ultimate revelation of God, for He is the express image of His person. Christ's human nature is what God would be like if He were clothed in flesh. His humanity is not God, but is united to God forever. God's anger at Christ's cross therefore is not revelation of an emotion of God akin to man's anger, but rather it is the expression, the revelation of His pure and holy nature which is infinite in being.

Jesus is mankind fully clothed and in its right mind.

The Quiet Waters By

We've just considered (above) something of who Jesus is as a Person. We have noted that the Bible teaches that Jesus is one divine Person with two natures forever. As Man He can identify with our sufferings.[17] And as God He can help and even heal us.[18] "Then Jesus said, 'Come to Me, all of you who are weary and carry heavy burdens, and I will give you rest.'"[19]

Now, they say that music soothes the savage beast.[20] Songs remind us of good times/bad times. Having been a Christian now for many years I find that hymns tend to come to mind in times of trouble. Though the R.E.M. song

---

[17] Therefore, since we have a great High Priest who has ascended into heaven, Jesus the Son of God, let us hold firmly to the faith we profess. For we do not have a High Priest who is unable to empathize with our weaknesses, but we have one who has been tempted in every way, just as we are-yet He did not sin." Hebrews 4:14-15.

[18] At that very time Jesus cured many who had diseases, sicknesses and evil spirits, and gave sight to many who were blind." Luke 7:21.

[19] Matthew 11:28. The New Living Translation of the Bible.

[20] "'Music has Charms to soothe a savage Breast.' The phrase was coined by the Playwright/Poet William Congreve, in The Mourning Bride, 1697: ACT I. SCENE I. A Room of State." (Internet)

"Everybody Hurts" did help me to get through a particularly dark and difficult period.

Whenever I was about to teach the two-day ASIST (Applied Suicide Intervention Skills Training) Course, that song would invariably start playing in my head. However, at best, the song only tells us not to throw in our hand but to hold on by taking comfort in your friends because everybody cries and everybody hurts sometimes. Like I say, the song helped me through one of the darkest periods in my life. I am thankful to the song and its authors for that. However, it was Jesus who sustained me and healed me. He removed all the bitterness and anger I was experiencing at that time, bitterness and anger towards those who were seeking the demise of me, my family and my livelihood!

The following hymn (especially the *refrain*) was also included in the 'music loop' that constantly played in my head as I walked through the valley of the shadow of death.

> O soul, are you weary and troubled?
> No light in the darkness you see?
> There's light for a look at the Saviour,
> And life more abundant and free!
> *Refrain:*
> Turn your eyes upon Jesus,
> Look full in His wonderful face,
> And the things of earth will grow strangely dim,
> In the light of His glory and grace.[21]

It is Jesus alone who brings us comfort, true and lasting comfort. The beauty of it is that we encounter Him (who is the Word) in His Word the Bible. No visions or voices are required. He simply speaks to us in the quietness of our

---

[21] Hymn by Helen H. Lemmel (1864-1961).

heart. He speaks to us when we meditate and ruminate on His Word. However, we must acknowledge that it is His Word as we talk to Him. How will we know that it is not an imposter if we listen to something or someone other than God speaking in His Word? Therefore, to ensure you have the correct Jesus you must test everything against His written Word, i.e., the sixty-six books of the Bible. And remember that "It is impossible to please God without faith. Anyone who wants to come to Him must believe that God exists and that He rewards those who sincerely seek Him."[22]

As you seek to draw near to Him keep the words of *The Shepherd's Psalm*, Psalm 23 in mind, "He leadeth me beside the still waters." An intimate encounter with Jesus could take place anywhere. However, a troubled heart and a busy mind can be calmed and stilled simply by pondering the quiet flow of a river. Keep in mind what the Bible says about who Jesus is in relation to you and to God, "For there is one God and one mediator between God and mankind, the man Christ Jesus." 1 Timothy 2:5, and what Jesus says, "No one comes to the Father except through me." John 14:6b.

Jesus often took time out to be alone, to get away from the crowds. He sought quiet times in quiet places. Therefore, because Jesus is a frequenter of quiet places, you have a better opportunity of meeting Him at one of these. A spiritual encounter with Jesus includes words as well as feelings. And because it is spiritual it remains invisible. For it is a heart to heart dialogue that takes place in the mind.

Let me try to illustrate how we may connect or reconnect with God. We can become so tied up with our own busyness that we don't realise that we're neglecting our relationship with God.

_____

[22] Hebrews 11:6. New Living Translation.

"You need to take time out to de-stress. Go for a walk on a beach. Feel the sand between your toes." Thus said the doctor to me during a conversation I had as I was sprinting toward the end of a very busy year. I skidded to a halt. She had stopped me in my tracks: "Stress? What? As an Army Chaplain?" "Yes, you have a stressful job." I'm still in a bit of denial here, but doctor knows best! Well, I suppose I had been very busy, what, with holding down a fulltime job and at the same time writing a graphic novel based on a true story.

More than three months had passed since the doctor told me to take that break. During the intervening period, I had spent many days in hospital on three different occasions. However, none of it was related to stress. It was twice for surgery and once to be treated for a raging kidney infection, morphine included! No walk on a beach. No sand between my toes. Only catheters and cannulas.

One of the plusses of having older brothers is that they have a special affection for their younger siblings. I have two older brothers. They have been giving valuable feedback on my novel – and my health. Should I try to make a blockbuster out of my novel as my publisher was gently suggesting? Would my health adversely suffer from the extra work this would entail? Says my eldest brother,

> I'm sorry to hear your health is not optimum, and particularly regarding the stress bit... Take the break your doctor is recommending. Wait upon the Lord. What does your Lord want you to do about this [blockbuster novel] option? A touch of Elijah here. Rest, sleep, eat, rest, sleep, eat. Tune into the horizon. Wait for that still small voice... Listen to the Lord. He walked away from the crowds. Do nothing

without Him. Bivouac, rest, wait for Spirit-touched intuition.

My love to you brother. Look after yourself, emotionally as well as physically. Even the birds on the branches are imbued by God with the blessed healing instinct to have a bath in a puddle, preen and oil the feathers, enjoy the sun for a while, eat well, fly happily within God-given capacities. No shame in that. Never shame in that. It is fulfilment. It is Ecclesiastes. God is the only audience, the only readership, whose endorsement ultimately matters. – Fergie.

"Listen to the Lord. He walked away from the crowds." Wow! Jesus sought no adulating crowds. He sought no man's praise! Often I've sung the following words of *Be Thou My Vision*, that ancient Irish hymn that speaks to the Celt in me:

Riches I need not, nor man's empty praise,
Thou mine inheritance, now and always:
Thou and Thou only, first in my heart
High King of heaven, my treasure Thou art.[23]

"Crowds of people came to hear Him and to be healed of their sickness. But Jesus often withdrew to lonely places and prayed." Luke 5:15b-16. (See also Matthew 14:13; Mark 1:35; 6:45-46; Luke 22:41 etc.)

Far from the Madding Crowd was a popular Thomas Hardy novel written in 1874 and turned into a movie in

---

[23] Sung to the tune *Slane*, Ancient Irish, *tr.* by Mary Byrne, 1880-1931; versified by Eleanor Hull, 1860-1935. The Scottish Psalter 1929 Metrical Version and Scripture Paraphrases, Oxford University Press, London, Glasgow, New York, 1929.

1915; 1967; 1998 and 2015. Hardy borrowed his book's title from the 1751 poem *Elegy Written in a Country Churchyard:*

> Far from the Madding crowd's ignoble strife
> Their sober wishes never learn'd to stray,
> Along the cool sequester'd vale of life
> They kept the noiseless tenor of their way.[24]

If Jesus needed to retreat from the frenzied crowds, then so do I – so do we all. But separately of course and not together! We need time to reflect; time to think; time to de-stress; time to pray.

I'd had three general anaesthetics in a one year. Each time, before they put me under, I would pray and try to think of Bible verses that applied to my situation. Invariably the versified form of Psalm 23, *The Lord's My Shepherd* would get stuck in my head, especially the fourth stanza which I would sing in my head to the tune *Crimond*:

> Yea, though I walk through death's dark vale,
> Yet will I fear none ill:
> For Thou art with me; And Thy rod
> And staff me comfort still.[25]

"Yea, though I walk through death's dark vale..." They had pumped me full of morphine and I watched the ceiling lights flash by as they wheeled me on a gurney into the Intensive Care Unit. "What? Morphine. ICU? Wasn't my dad when he was dying pumped full of morphine in an Intensive Care Unit?" I didn't want to be alone, to die alone.

---

[24] Thomas Gray.

[25] Stanza 4, Psalm 23, *The Psalms and Church Hymnary (Revised Edition) 1927.*

I wanted my wife and family, my grandchildren at my bedside, just as it was for my dad. However, I was stressing about nothing. I was in the ICU, not because I was dying, but because there was nowhere else to put me at that time. Next morning they moved me to another room two floors above. Phew!

Meanwhile, back to my "blockbuster" novel. My second eldest brother Stuart had just finished reading it. Says Stuart:

> Obviously a mega-work, with so many strands of human experience; of societal development with brutality always in the next room to genteel parlour chit-chat. What is truth, the book demands, and yet more, Who is Truth? I'm off for a walk along the River Kelvin to think about this again.

The River Kelvin is in Glasgow, *The Dear Green Place*, whose motto is, "Let Glasgow flourish through the preaching of Thy Word and praising Thy name." Shortened to *Let Glasgow Flourish* and stamped on Glasgow's coat of arms with its bell, tree, bird and fish. The motto was an inscription on a bell that was made in 1637 for the Tron Kirk, which church Stuart attended. Stuart was going for a walk along the Kelvin to think.

As I thought about Stuart walking along the banks of the River Kelvin I couldn't help but also think of the words of a song by Hue and Cry called *Mother Glasgow*.[26] It refers to Glasgow's Coat of Arms, the bell, tree, bird and fish rhyme, to "Billies and Tims"[27] (summing up the

---

[26] Hue and Cry (1989). Song and music by Michael Marra.
[27] Billies and Tims – Glaswegian reference to Protestants and a Roman Catholics respectively.

protestant/Catholic sectarianism that exists in Glasgow, albeit to a much lesser extent than when I lived and worked in its environs), of having a dander, i.e., a wee walk, with Glasgow's patron saint, St. Mungo (or Kentigern), and trying to catch that fish that couldn't swim.

Stuart was not trying to catch a fish that couldn't swim. Nor was he walking with St. Mungo. He was needing somewhere quiet to go, somewhere where he could think. The banks of the River Kelvin fitted the bill.

Even Scotland's national bard spent contemplatory time on the banks of a river as attested to by his poem *Ye Banks and Braes O' Bonnie Doon*:

> Oft hae I roved by bonnie Doon
> To see the rose and woodbine twine
> And ilka bird sang o' its love
> And fondly sae did I o' mine.[28]

We all need to retreat from the hurly-burly from time to time, far from the madding crowd. What better place than the River Kelvin in Glasgow *The Dear Green Place?* In solitude we walk with you Stuart, with you in spirit, as you dander, not with St. Mungo, but with the Lord.

> The Lord's my Shepherd, I'll not want,
> He makes me down to lie
> In pastures green: He leadeth me
> The quiet waters by.[29]

---

[28] Robert Burns.

[29] Stanza 2, Psalm 23, *The Psalms and Church Hymnary (Revised Edition) 1927.*

What happens at "the quiet waters by"? The start of the very next verse says, "My soul He doth restore again..." Soul-restoration! That's what a quiet walk beside a river can get you – soul-restoration. It's a place where we can reflect, a place where we can recalibrate,

> By Babel's streams we sat and wept,
> When Sion we thought on.
> In midst thereof we hang'd our harps
> The willow-trees upon...
> O how the Lord's song shall we sing
> Within a foreign land?
> If thee, Jerus'lem, I forget,
> Skill part from my right hand.[30]

And here's Burns again with a faint echo of the exile's pain,

> Ye banks and braes o' bonnie Doon
> How can ye bloom sae fresh and fair?
> How can ye chant, ye little birds
> And I sae weary full o' care?
> Ye'll break my heart, ye warbling bird
> That wanton's thro' the flowering thorn
> Ye mind me o' departed joys
> Departed never to return.[31]

Departed joys? The hymnist William Cowper in his hymn *O For a Closer Walk with God* spoke of these:

---

[30] – from Psalm 137, *The Psalms and Church Hymnary (Revised Edition) 1927.*
[31] Robert Burns.

Return, O Holy Dove! Return,
Sweet messenger of rest!
I hate the sins that made Thee mourn,
And drove Thee from my breast.[32]

It was while He was by a river, the River Jordan that the Holy Spirit came upon Jesus: "Jesus also was baptised; and while He prayed the heaven was opened. And the Holy Spirit descended in bodily form like a dove upon Him..." Luke 3:22b.

Meanwhile back with Stuart by the River Kelvin, "He leadeth me the quiet waters by." Yes, the noise of the city gets drowned out by the quiet of the river. Wars in the breast cease when the Prince of Peace walks beside you. We beat our hate into love upon the anvil of His compassion. There our red hot anger gets turned into mercy by the hammer of His Word.

Lord Jesus be near me too. "My soul He doth restore again." Give me some of that soul-restoration!

The Shepherd Psalm

While driving to church one Sunday morning I was listening to a sermon on the radio about Psalm 23, "The Shepherd's Psalm." Let me post the beautiful, poetic and majestic King James' Version of that Psalm:,

1The LORD is my shepherd; I shall not want.
² He maketh me to lie down in green pastures: He leadeth me beside the still waters.
³ He restoreth my soul: He leadeth me in the paths of righteousness for His name's sake.

---

[32] Hymn 455, *The Psalms and Church Hymnary (Revised Edition) 1927.*

⁴Yea, though I walk through the valley of the shadow of death, I will fear no evil: for Thou art with me; Thy rod and Thy staff they comfort me.
⁵Thou preparest a table before me in the presence of mine enemies: Thou anointest my head with oil; my cup runneth over.
⁶Surely goodness and mercy shall follow me all the days of my life: and I will dwell in the house of the LORD for ever.

As I listened to the sermon on this text my mind wandered back to November 2005 when I had flown back to Scotland from Tasmania to be beside my dad who was on his deathbed at age 83. He had his eyes closed but he seemed to be listening intently to me as I told him how much I loved him and how much I appreciated how good a dad he had been to me as I was growing up.

I mentioned to him some of my happy memories, such as him taking us swimming at Dumbarton's Brock Baths in winter, Craig's Pool at Glen Fruin, as well as Loch Lomond at Balloch countless times in summer. I held his hand in mine as I spoke softly to him, knowing that these were his very last days on earth. At that moment he was the centre of my universe as I concentrated hard on finding the right words, though the words just seemed to bubble up from somewhere deep within and overflowed like the clear waters of Pappert Well.

Dad had been a committed Communist. (I had asked him point blank one time many years before if he was a Communist and was shocked when he had answered unequivocally in the affirmative!) To me Communism and Atheism were synonymous terms! He had worked in the Glasgow shipyards on the "Red Clydeside" and had mingled with those who wanted the workers of the world to unite!

Anyway, I couldn't understand how he had been happy to attend church on Sunday and even wax eloquent about doing the "reading" in church and telling us that the King James' Version of the Bible was the most beautiful, noble and poetic of all the versions of the Bible. He was as happy pulling the rope that rang the bell to beckon Sunday-worshippers to Jamestown Parish Church, part of the Church of Scotland.

"Dad, you know Psalm 23? The Lord is my Shepherd? Are you able to say those words – 'the Lord is MY Shepherd'? Is He YOUR Shepherd? Is Jesus your SHEPHERD? He says He's the Good Shepherd? Are you trusting in Him even now? 'Yea, though I walk in death's dark vale, yet will I fear none ill, for Thou art with me; and Thy rod and staff me comfort still.'[33] Dad, trust Him. Trust Him even now dad. He'll look after you even now as you go through that dark valley."

I prayed with my dad, I prayed *for* him, asking that my God, our God would look after him. Did my dad actually hear me say all of this? I believe so. But more importantly, God heard! I look forward to seeing my dad (and my mum) in glory...

Thank You Lord that I was able to be with my dad just before he died.

Does it matter whether we believe that Jesus is the Son of God or not? Well, it does when you're on your deathbed. The Bible says, "For the wages of sin is death, but the gift of God is eternal life in Christ Jesus our Lord." Romans 6:23. Dying therefore is God giving you the wages for your sin. Death came to the human race through Adam. "When Adam sinned, sin entered the world. Adam's sin brought death, so death spread to everyone, for everyone

---

[33] Revised Church Hymnal, Psalm 23.

sinned."[34] So, to receive wages is to receive what you have earned, but the Good News is that "the gift of God is eternal life in Christ Jesus our Lord."

The Son of God is God's gift to us. For in Him alone is the gift of salvation. No belief in the Son of God means no life, no everlasting life. It means only death and judgment. "Whoever believes in the Son of God accepts this testimony. Whoever does not believe God has made Him out to be a liar, because they have not believed the testimony God has given about His Son. And this is the testimony: God has given us eternal life, and this life is in His Son. Whoever has the Son has life; whoever does not have the Son of God does not have life. I write these things to you who believe in the name of the Son of God so that you may know that you have eternal life." 1 John 5:10-13.

God's gift of everlasting life is free. We don't have to work for it, or even try to work for it. It is a gift. Gifts, as you know, are free. God's gift of eternal life is free because it has been paid for already. If it has been paid for already it means that we cannot do anything to earn it. We can add nothing to Christ's cross (except our applause)! Will you applaud the Son of God by believing in Him?

Faith Comes by Hearing

Jesus, the Son of God, is the Shepherd. But He is not just any old shepherd. He is the Good Shepherd. And what does this Good Shepherd say about His sheep? "My sheep hear My voice, and I know them, and they follow Me. And I give them eternal life, and they shall never perish; neither shall anyone snatch them out of My hand. My Father, who has given *them* to Me, is greater than all; and no one is able

---

[34] Romans 5:12, The New Living Translation.

to snatch *them* out of My Father's hand. I and *My* Father are one."[35]

The Good Shepherd's sheep *hear* His voice. He knows them and they *follow* Him. Jesus spoke those words to a group of people who did not believe that He was the promised Messiah, the Christ. He said to them, "You do not believe, because you are not My sheep"[36] Jesus knows who His sheep are. As much as it is good to know Jesus, it is far better to be known by Him. For who wants to hear Him say, "I never knew you. Away from me, you evildoers!"[37]

How do we hear the voice of Jesus? How do we get to know Jesus? Well, the answer is, "Faith comes by hearing, and hearing by the Word of God"[38] What is the Word of God? "All Scripture is God-breathed and is useful for teaching, rebuking, correcting and training in righteousness, so that the servant of God may be thoroughly equipped for every good work."[39] So we see then that we hear the voice of the Good Shepherd in all the Scriptures from Genesis 1:1 to Revelation 22:21. Jesus is the Word incarnated. The Bible is the Word inscripturated. The latter reveals the former. It is how Christians hear His voice. And Jesus says, "He who enters by the door is the shepherd of the sheep. To him the doorkeeper opens, and the sheep hear his voice; and he calls his own sheep by name and leads them out. And when he brings out his own sheep, he goes before them; and the sheep follow him, for they know his voice. Yet they will by no means follow a stranger, but will flee from him, for they do not know the voice of strangers"[40]

---

[35] John 10:27-30 NKJV.
[36] John 10:26a NKJV.
[37] Matthew 7:23b NIV.
[38] Romans 10:17 NKJV.
[39] 2 Timothy 3:16-17 NIV.
[40] John 10:2-5 NKJV.

As a young teenager, when I knew Jesus only as a swear word, I kept homing pigeons. The pigeon loft was located in a grassy clearing next to the ruins of Tullichewan Castle. There was also a farmhouse with a cobbled courtyard that had once been the stables for the castle. At night, some friends and I would occasionally get together in the pigeon hut to try to contact the dead through the means of a home-made Ouija board. We called it "Spirit in the Glass." Each member was to breathe into the glass. Then we would place the whisky glass rim down on the board upon which each letter of the alphabet was laid out along with the numbers 0 to 9 and a "YES" and "NO" at opposite sides of the board. Each member would place an index fingertip on the bottom of the inverted glass. "Spirit of the glass are you with us?" This question would be asked until the glass started to move. Invariably there would be accusations that someone was pushing the glass and as many denials. The glass would spell out the name of the supposed spirit we had contact with. Next time we'll put butter on the glass so that no one will be able to push the glass without their finger sliding off!

And so it was. Our theory was that the body heat from our fingers on the glass caused the air in it to expand and thus, like a hovercraft, the glass would glide across the board. But what about the spirit spelling out names and answering questions? Well, if no one was able to push the glass because of the melting butter (we also tried Vaseline), then what was going on? Sometimes the glass would just have a life of its own, spelling out answers to our questions even when no fingers were on the glass! Creepy? You bet!

The scariest time was when the glass began speedily and erratically spelling out on its own, what we thought was, "I am good." "What?" we responded, "You are good?" "No!" came the quick answer, "I am God!" At that, even though there were no fingers upon it, the glass flew off the board and hit the wall!

Other than scare the living daylights out of me, my experience with Ouija boards also opened my mind up to the possibility, nay probability or even actuality of another dimension, an invisible, spiritual realm. Sure, we tried to rationalise it all away, and sure, it is all subjective experience on my part, but this spirit business became real to me. Indeed, I could write a book on the ghost stories and weird experiences I began having around that time. However, the point is that whether I was "hearing the voice" of an actual dead person or the voice of a demon impersonating an actual dead person when the glass spelled out words, I became aware of the supernatural. From there, though it was almost two decades later, I began to think that if there was a spirit realm, then maybe God who is Spirit needs to be investigated. So I joined a Masonic Lodge[41] thinking that maybe God was hiding in there, in among all their "secret" activities.

I used to write research papers for my local Masonic Lodge and subsequently they gave me an award for doing so. Part of the award included a King James' Version of the Bible – which I read. One needs to be careful (I say this tongue-in-cheek) when one reads the Bible, lest one be converted! There was one verse of the Bible in particular that led to my being converted by the Author of the Book, John 14:6, the second half of the verse in particular. I've written about this elsewhere, so here's a quote from my From Mason To Minister book:

> Not everyone is converted to Christianity the same way as the Pharisee Saul of Tarsus on the road to

---

[41] The Ancient Free and Accepted Masons

Damascus. Saul, of course, became Paul the Apostle of Jesus Christ. Indeed some children grow up in Christian homes never knowing the moment of their conversion, knowing only that they have always loved Jesus and have always trusted in Him alone for salvation. In some ways I envy those Christians.

My own conversion was climactic. Like a stuck needle on an old broken record, I was trying to come to grips with Jesus saying, "I am the way, the truth, and the life. No one comes to the Father except through Me" (John 14:6). I thought this exclusivity was very arrogant. I remember sitting in my armchair contemplating these words, and wondering who this Jesus thought He was! The "stone the builders rejected" of the Bible (and of the Chapter of the Royal Arch teaching) was about to really sink into and permanently lodge in my heart.

My brother Fearghas' painting of the spaceman lost in space became how I felt. He had become detached from the mother ship – I was lost in space. The millions of stars were twinkling in the black night sky. I was surrounded by people at work and had my family at home. I played soccer. I had a busy social life. I attended Masonic meetings, but like the drifting spaceman, I began to feel so lonely and detached in the universe. Still, in my heart I pondered the things I had learned about God as I sat on my armchair.

I began to call out to God audibly: "I want to know You!" I had come to the stage in my philosophical travels of being unable to prove to myself whether I was awake or dreaming. It's a terribly terrifying place to be, not knowing if I was dreaming that reality is real, or worse, whether I was part of someone else's dream! How does anyone know if they really exist? How are we to measure reality? Perhaps I was really in a coma lying on a hospital bed somewhere.

Is truth a subjective thing? If it is, then, am I the measure of reality? Am I the centre of the universe? Does the universe cabalistically emanate from me as its centre? (I had delved into cabalism as I fossicked around in the dusty tomes of Masonic literature in Masonic libraries.)

For there to be objective truth there would need to be a Supreme Being Who had revealed His will to man. Otherwise one man's opinion is as valid as any other man's contradiction.

I believed in a Supreme Being, but who was He? I continued to cry out to Him. And as I did so, I listened in my heart for the answer. But all that I could hear was Jesus saying I am the way, the truth, and the life. No one comes to the Father except through Me. I would reply to Him, "Get out of my way. I am looking for God!" And again I would cry out to God. And again Jesus would say, No one comes to the Father except through Me. Around and around we would go. Sitting alone in that armchair I became, in my mind, the spaceman. The severed umbilical cord slowly flapped in the solar wind. The stars in the dark sky continued silently blinking. I began to gasp for air. I felt weak. I gasped for God, for life! "I want to know You, God!" No one comes to the Father except through Me was the singular reply. "But I'm looking for God!"

Then it happened. The lights went out in my mind. Not one twinkling star in the black expanse of the universe – only utter darkness! Horror and great darkness fell upon me! Like a fish in a net, or deep in the dark hold of the icy bowels of a fisherman's boat, I feebly gasped for air! "I want to know God!" My cry was very feeble now. Again the words of Jesus entered my mind: I am the way, the truth, and the life. No one comes to the Father except through Me.

Tears began to stream down my face when at last I realized who Jesus is. He is God! How stupid of me! I had seen it over and over in the Bible, yet it never really dawned on me until I was at the end of my tether. Jesus is my Saviour. He is my Lord and my God. As I sat in my armchair, I began to cling to Him for dear life. And it was only afterward that I recognized that He was the One who held me safely in His grip first. By His Spirit, working with His Word, the Father had revealed the Son to me. The Spirit enabled me to see the Father in the Son, Jesus Christ. Jesus is the way to God. He is the Truth. He is objective truth – truth outside of me, outside of all men. And He is the Life – everlasting life. Jesus is Paradise. He is Noah's Ark. He is Solomon's Temple. He is Salvation. 'Though the fig tree may not blossom, nor fruit be on the vines; though the labor of the olive may fail, and the fields yield no food; though the flock may be cut off from the fold, and there be no herd in the stalls – yet I will rejoice in the Lord, I will joy in the God of my salvation. The Lord God [i.e., Jehovah Adonai] is my strength; He will make my feet like deer's feet, and He will make me walk on my high hills.' (Hab. 3:17-19)

> There came a Shepherd long ago,
> Searching for His sheep.
> He will not rest till all His flock

Is safely in His keep.
With open arms He calls to them.
His voice is soft yet clear.
And they come home to Him again.
The Shepherd loves them dear.
Good Shepherd I will heed Your call,
For this I must confess:
I cannot find my own way out
Of this darkened wilderness. – Author[42]

The Bible

If we are going to listen only to God and not to dead people and/or demons spelling out sentences on Ouija boards, then which version of the Bible ought we to use? Yes, I suppose it might be easier if we could hear voices and see visions, but we believe those ways of God revealing Himself are long gone, especially since He has given us the sixty-six books of the Bible.

Like the Triune God, the Bible is one but many. The many books are one book. And, reflecting the two natures of Christ, who is 100% God and 100% Man, the Bible is 100% written by God and 100% written by men: "For prophecy never had its origin in the human will, but prophets, though human, spoke from God as they were carried along by the Holy Spirit."[43] This was no automatic writing. These men wrote what they wanted to write and, as it happens, they wrote what the Holy Spirit wanted them to write. If you have ever got 10/10 in an exam, then so did the writers of each of the sixty-six book that make up the Bible.

[42] From Mason To Minister *Through the Lattice*, Nordskog Publishing Inc., Ventura, California 2011, pp, 98-100.
[43] 2 Peter 1:21-22 NIV.

Now, it goes without saying that not everyone believes that the Bible is the Word of God, i.e., His revelation to human beings. This is something that only the Holy Spirit can convince you of. I can't! The Spirit always works with the Word. That is how God speaks to us. God does not speak to us by upturned whisky glasses on Ouija Boards. Rather, God speaks to us by His Spirit working with His Word. But again, not everyone believes that the Bible is the actual Word of God inscripturated.

I heard a song on the car radio as I was driving to church on a recent Sunday morning. I had just listened to a mediocre sermon about love. Then the station started playing, what they call, "Christian Rock Music," most of which I do not like. So, I switched to the station whose music I do like. The one where they play all the oldies. Anyway, ironically the song on my Oldies Station was an annoying put-down of the Bible. It is called "It Ain't Necessarily So" which has been done by various artists over the years since George and Ira Gershwin wrote it for their Porgy and Bess opera in 1935. In the opera the song is sung by the character Sportin' Life, a seedy drug dealer, who tells us about his doubt about some statements in the Bible.

> It ain't necessarily so
> It ain't necessarily so
> De things dat yo' liable to read in de Bible
> It ain't necessarily so.[44]

Now, I remember someone asking me if I believed all that Jonah in the belly of a whale stuff. It was a great question to ask me at that time. I had just begun to study the Bible for myself. I had tried to read it a couple of times

---

[44] George & Ira Gershwin, Porgy and Bess, 1935.

before but had got stuck at Leviticus after I had read through Genesis then Exodus when I was sixteen or so. The next time I don't even think I made it through Genesis. Anyway, in my early thirties I managed, with great difficulty, to read the entire Bible that the Masonic Lodge had presented me. I had the King James' Version (KJV) of the Bible in one hand and a dictionary in the other! I found ye olde English contained therein really hard to understand. I mentioned already that my dad's favourite version of the Bible was the King James' Version. He thought that it was the most beautiful, noble and poetic of all the versions of the Bible. My brother Stuart wrote the following to me:

> Faither so often quoted Isaiah, freely from memory, as we drove to somewhere for lunch up Loch Lomondside. I have his marked Bibles from which he delivered readings to the congregation at Jamestown Parish Church, with me and Mum sitting half-way up on the left while he did in all humility take his place at the lectern and read... I loved him for that, oh, how I loved him for that.[45]

Regardless of what my dad thought of the King James Version of the Bible, I found the archaisms that it's full of, hard to understand. So, the moral of the tale is that you should try to get a version of the Bible that has been written in your own language. I've dipped into Scottish Gaelic, Scots (Lallans), French, Koine Greek and ancient Hebrew versions. However, even though I've read cover to cover the New International Version, the English Standard Version, and large chunks of other versions (e.g., the New American Standard Version), I must admit that my default

---

[45] Stuart in an email to me dated 27 March 2016.

version is the New King James Version. However, you will notice that so far I have been quoting mainly from the NIV and the New Living Translation. This is simply to keep things in line with the title of this book, Jesus For the Layman.

Meanwhile, back to Jonah and the whale. Well, for a start the original language of the Hebrew portion of the Bible (i.e., the Old Testament) doesn't say that a whale swallowed Jonah. Rather it was a great fish. But, be that as it may, who could believe such a thing could occur? Who could believe that a fish could vomit up a human being onto some beach and then that human being could walk around and call on a whole city (Nineveh) to repent so as to avoid God's impending judgment upon that city? Well, do I believe what the Bible says about Jonah being swallowed by a fish? Yes! And so does Jesus. "For as Jonah was three days and three nights in the belly of a huge fish, so the Son of Man will be three days and three nights in the heart of the earth."[46] But what does Sportin' Life, the seedy drug dealer, in the Porgy and Bess opera have to say about Jonah (and David and Moses for that matter)?

> Li'l David was small but oh my
> Li'l David was small but oh my
> He fought big Goliath who lay down and dieth
> Li'l David was small but oh my
> Oh Jonah he lived in de whale
> Oh Jonah he lived in de whale
> For he made his home in dat fish's abdomen
> Oh Jonah he lived in de whale
> Li'l Moses was found in a stream
> Li'l Moses was found in a stream
> He floated on water 'til ole Pharaoh's daughter

---

[46] Matthew 12:40 NIV.

She fished him she says from that stream
It ain't necessarily so
It ain't necessarily so.

I think I'd much rather believe God speaking in Scripture than some singer in an opera. At least I can check out the Bible for myself. That's why a good version that you can understand is essential. Scholars debate which is the best and most accurate translation of the original texts into English. But for the sake of keeping it simple, I would recommend the New International Version as a place for the layman to start.

Now, remember that I said that I cannot convince you that the Bible is the actual Word of God. Only God Himself can do that. Indeed, only God Himself can convince you that He exists. He does use means, such as people and events. However, from the Book of Isaiah from which my dad so often quoted so "freely and from memory" which is to say, in the words of my dad's favourite version the Bible, "To the law and to the testimony: if they speak not according to this word, it is because there is no light in them." Or, as the easier to understand New Living Translation renders the Hebrew into modern English, "Look to God's instructions and teachings! People who contradict his word are completely in the dark."[47]

One of the best ways of understanding the Bible is to take everything back to the beginning. In the Vale of Leven when I was growing up there were two movie theatres (or picture hooses as we called them, viz., the Strand and the Hall). You could come in half way through a film and wait for the "second showing." The same movie would be shown again. However, if you start watching a

---

[47] Isaiah 8:20.

movie half way through, then you're left trying to guess what happened beforehand. This is what a lot of people do with the Bible. Like fish-gut at the bottom of a tackle box, they get into some real tangles. Jonah and the Whale is one of them. However, like everything else in the Bible, take it back to the start. Where did evil come from? Take it back to Genesis. Where did death come from? Take it back to Genesis. Where did lying come from? Take it back to Genesis. I'm sure you're getting the picture. Where did the sun, the moon, the earth and stars come from? Take it back to Genesis. Where did you and I (and fish and whales) come from? Take it back to Genesis. What does the opening verse of the Bible say? "In the beginning God created the heavens and the earth (Genesis 1:1). The point I make is that if God can create all of creation and all therein out of nothing, then Jonah in the belly of a fish is easy for Him, as is the virgin birth, the resurrection and all the other miracles listed in the Bible. God speaks and things that are not become things that are. Nothing is too hard for God. So, don't listen anyone who does not speak according to Scripture. And if they do, then check it out for yourself. Be like the Bereans. "Now the Berean Jews were of more noble character than those in Thessalonica, for they received the message with great eagerness and examined the Scriptures every day to see if what Paul said was true."[48] But don't be like Sportin' Life, the drug dealer. Don't believe him when he says,

> Dey tell all you chillun de debble's a villain
> But 'taint necessarily so
> To get into Hebben don' snap for a sebben
> Live clean, don' have no fault
> Oh I takes dat gospel whenever it's pos'ble

---

[48] Acts 17:11 NIV.

But wid a grain of salt
Methus'lah lived nine hundred years
Methus'lah lived nine hundred years
But who calls dat livin' when no gal'll give in
To no man what's nine hundred years
I'm preachin' dis sermon to show
It ain't nessa, ain't nessa
Ain't nessa, ain't nessa
It ain't necessarily so.

Like me, as you read the lyrics of It Ain't Necessarily So, you no doubt found the language a little bit difficult to understand; "Chillun", "debble", "Hebben" and "sebben" etc. The point I make is therefore why struggle through a version of the Bible written in archaic language when there are more contemporary English versions?

"Gin ye confess wi your mouth at Jesus is Lord, an trew in your hairt at God raised him frae the deid, ye will be saufed." Romans 10:9, The New Testament in Scots.

"That if thou shalt confess with thy mouth the LORD Jesus, and shalt believe in thine heart that God hath raised him from the dead, thou shalt be saved." Romans 10:9, King James Version (KJV).

"That if you confess with your mouth the Lord Jesus and believe in your heart that God has raised Him from the dead, you will be saved." New King James Version (NKJV).

"If you declare with your mouth, 'Jesus is LORD,' and believe in your heart that God raised him from the dead, you will be saved." Romans 10:9, New International Version (NIV).

The idea then, is that you, as a layman, find a version that is easy for *you* to understand. Stick to the New International Version (NIV) or the New King James Version (NKJV), and yes, there are other good versions. But keep in mind that there are some not so good versions too!

Oh, and just before we conclude this chapter, let me remind you of an old nursery rhyme that we used to recite with accompanying hand actions as children in Scotland. We called it *Two Little Chookie Birds.* However, let's use the official version:

Two little dickie birds sitting on a wall,
One named Peter.
One named Paul.
Fly away Peter.
Fly away Paul.
Come back Peter.
Come back Paul.

Apparently when this rhyme was first recorded in 1765 in *Mother Goose's Memories* it started off:

There were two blackbirds
Sat upon a hill,
The one was nam'd Jack,
The other nam'd Gill.

It reminds me of the rhyme *Jack and Jill went up the hill* that was first published in 1777. However, the point I make is that the Jack and Gill names in time were replaced by the names of two of the Lord's Apostles, Peter and Paul. Paul wrote thirteen of the New Testament's twenty seven Books (fourteen if he also wrote Hebrews). Peter wrote two

New Testament Books, 1 and 2 Peter. Peter speaks of Paul in 2 Peter where he says,

> Bear in mind that our Lord's patience means salvation, just as our dear brother Paul also wrote you with the wisdom that God gave him. He writes the same way in all his letters, speaking in them of these matters. His letters contain some things that are hard to understand, which ignorant and unstable people distort, as they do the other Scriptures, to their own destruction.[49]

Notice two things that Peter says: one of Paul and the other of the Scriptures. Notice that Peter is calling Paul's letters "Scriptures." He includes Pauls writings (all thirteen or fourteen Books) as helping to make up the sixty six Books of the Bible. But notice that even Peter is admitting that Paul's letters "contain some things that are hard to understand." Therefore, it's not just the Biblical language that can be hard to understand, but also Biblical concepts. But here's a helpful tip from an old book first published in 1647, i.e., *The Westminster Confession of Faith*:

> Not all things in Scripture are equally plain in themselves or equally clear to all; yet those things which are necessary to be known, believed, and observed for salvation are so clearly stated and explained in one place or another in Scripture, that not only the educated but also the uneducated may gain a sufficient understanding of them by a proper use of the ordinary means.
>
> The Old Testament in Hebrew (which was the native language of the people of God of old) and the New

---

[49] 2 Peter 3:15-16 NIV.

Testament in Greek (which at the time it was written was the language most generally known to the nations), being directly inspired by God and by His unique care and providence kept pure in all ages, are therefore authoritative, so that in all controversies of religion the church is finally to appeal to them. But, because these original languages are not understood by all the people of God, who have a right to, and a vital interest in, the Scriptures and are commanded to read and search them in the fear of God, therefore the Scriptures are to be translated into the common language of every nation to which they come; so that, the Word of God dwelling abundantly in all. They may worship Him in an acceptable manner and by perseverance and the encouragement of the Scriptures may have hope.

The infallible rule of interpretation of Scripture is the Scripture itself. Therefore, when there is a question about the true and full meaning of any Scripture (which is not manifold, but one), that meaning must be searched out and ascertained by other places that speak more clearly.

The supreme judge by whom all controversies of religion are to be settled and all decrees of councils, opinions of ancient writers, doctrines of men, and claims to private revelations are to be examined, can be only the Holy Spirit speaking in the Scripture. With His decisions we are to be satisfied.[50]

---

[50] *Westminster Confession of Faith* in the form adopted by the Orthodox Presbyterian Church (USA), with Parallel Modern English Study Version (MESV) 1993, Chapter 1, The Holy Scripture, paragraphs 7-10.

So we see then that Peter may be used to interpret Paul and Paul Peter. And that both Peter and Paul can be used to interpret other portions of Scripture or vice versa. For "The infallible rule of interpretation of Scripture is the Scripture itself." So, come back Peter and come back Paul. And may we never tell you to fly away!

Which Church?

As a new arrival from Canada to Australia and as a recent convert to Christianity I set out to find a suitable church to start to attend. I must admit that I didn't know too much about Denominations. I had become a Christian about maybe two years before I left the snowy Canadian winters for sunny Queensland. In Canada I had visited various churches not really being aware of which each Denomination was. I simply wanted to be a Christian without a label. I started attending what was called "a non-Denominational" church. Someone asked me which church I attended. When I told them that it was a non-Denominational church the response was, "So, you are a non-Denominationalist?" You can't win! Every Christian has a label, or at least every other Christian has a label for you. Therefore, I suggest that you don't worry so much about labels but concern yourself about attending a church in which God's Word is highly honoured and taught.

On my first Sunday morning in Australia I attended a church that was more interested in the voices and visions that they may (or may not!) have heard and seen, than the actual Word of God written. The next Sunday morning saw me in a Chinese church! The service was conducted in Cantonese with an English translator. God's Word was highly honoured but I thought they were translating what was being spoken in Chinese solely for my benefit!

Therefore, I thought I'd do that church a big favour by not attending again so that they could get on with things in their own language!

The following Sunday I found myself in church full of Dutch people. The service was conducted fully in English. Before the service began I was given a hymn-book at the front of which contained what is known as The Heidelberg Catechism. A Catechism, if you don't know, is "a summary of the principles of Christian religion in the form of questions and answers, used for the instruction of Christians."[51] The Heidelberg Catechism begins with,

Lord's Day 1

Q & A 1
Q. What is your only comfort in life and in death?

A. That I am not my own,[1] but belong— body and soul, in life and in death—[2] to my faithful Savior, Jesus Christ.[3] He has fully paid for all my sins with his precious blood,[4] and has set me free from the tyranny of the devil.[5] He also watches over me in such a way[6] that not a hair can fall from my head without the will of my Father in heaven;[7] in fact, all things must work together for my salvation.[8] Because I belong to him, Christ, by his Holy Spirit, assures me of eternal life[9] and makes me wholeheartedly willing and ready from now on to live for him.[10]

[1] 1 Cor. 6:19-20
[2] Rom. 14:7-
[3] 1 Cor. 3:23; Titus 2:14
[4] 1 Pet. 1:18-19; 1 John 1:7-9; 2:2
[5] John 8:34-36; Heb. 2:14-15; 1 John 3:1-11

---

[51] Internet.

[6] John 6:39-40; 10:27-30; 2 Thess. 3:3; 1 Pet. 1:5
[7] Matt. 10:29-31; Luke 21:16-18
[8] Rom. 8:28
[9] Rom. 8:15-16; 2 Cor. 1:21-22; 5:5; Eph. 1:13-14
[10] Rom. 8:1-17

I asked one of the elders if I could take a copy of their hymnbook (containing the Catechism) home with me to study and that I'd bring it back the following Sunday. My request was granted and I studied the Heidelberg Catechism cover to cover! Like a good Berean, for the whole week I checked everything therein again and again against Scripture. This church used the New International Version of which I had a copy.

I attended that church each Sunday morning thereafter and eventually got baptised there and became a member. The Bible was faithfully expounded from the pulpit each Sunday as we worshipped God.

Not only do I hold The Heidelberg Catechism in high esteem for teaching what the Scriptures say in an easy to understand and pastoral way, but I would endorse also The Westminster Larger Catechism and the more easily digestible Westminster Shorter Catechism. These are wonderful teaching aids in that they succinctly summarise what the Bible says about each question asked. Westminster Shorter Catechism Q & A 1, What is the chief end of man? Ans. Man's chief end is to glorify God and enjoy Him forever. (1 Corinthians 10:31; Romans 11:36).

So, the layman should find a reliable version of the Bible. He/she should read and study the Bible. He/she should find a church that honours and expounds the Bible. He/she should check out against the Bible the things that the church is teaching. He/she should utilise The Heidelberg and Westminster Shorter Catechism (find them on-line) to help him/her to get an easy and helpful handle on the basic things the Bible is teaching. Should the layman do these things diligently, not only will he/she simply believe that Jesus is Lord. He/she will be honouring and serving Him as his/her Lord.

"Who Do You Say I Am?"

I started my working life as an apprentice Marine Plumber in a Glasgow shipyard. I was fifteen going on sixteen when my dad, a boilermaker/plater, asked me what I was going to do when I left school. I just sort of shrugged and grunted whenever he asked me these types of questions. My eldest brother had become an art teacher and my second eldest a journalist. "I'll get you a real job," said my dad. "I don't want you ending up like that pair of pansies!" (or words to that affect and said tongue-in-cheek). So, before I knew it I was sitting aptitude tests to see if I had the right stuff to work in the same shipyard as my dad. Apparently I did. So, as an apprentice Marine Plumber I learned how to bend big bore pipes using heating torches, arc-weld, gas weld, braze, burn and all that heavy industry stuff.

From there I went on to become a Domestic Plumber working on houses in the Vale of Leven, Scotland and Toronto, Canada. Then I became a Railway Pipefitter in Winnipeg, Canada. Upon subsequent arrival in Brisbane, Australia I began working on building sites as a plumber. Why am I telling you all of this? Well, it's merely to make a simple point. Whether Scotland, Canada or Australia the language is the same. No, I don't mean the English language, but rather the colourful use of profanity that, like a caulker's gun, reverberates throughout shipyards, railway yards and building sites.

Now, I wasn't sure whether I should be stopping my use of four letter words, but upon my conversion I could see clearly that I needed to stop using God's name(s) as a swear word. There it was, staring right back at me from Scripture, "Thou shalt not take the name of the LORD thy God in vain; for the LORD will not hold him guiltless that taketh his name in vain."[52] I found that my taking the LORD's name in vain (i.e., blasphemy) immediately disappeared from my vocabulary when I was converted (while in the Canadian Railway job). The use of four letter words followed somewhere behind like a caboose, and, like the caboose, eventually was done away with.

One would need to believe that Jesus is God the LORD if one would see the need to stop using His name as a swear word. Sure, lots of people try to tidy up their "act" from time to time by cutting down on their use of foul language. I think even the Scottish comedian Billy Connolly once tried this for five minutes! However, surely you can see that if you really believed that Jesus was Lord you wouldn't be taking His name in vain? You wouldn't be using His name as a curse word.

CS Lewis is usually credited with coming up with the trilemma argument about who Jesus is: Lunatic, Liar, or Lord? Or sometimes the question about who Jesus is is phrased like this, Mad, Bad or God? How do we answer this question? Should we run off and ask the site foreman? The shipyard or railyard supervisor? Anyway, let's have a wee look at a quote from CS Lewis before we try to answer that,

---

[52] The Third Commandment as found in Exodus 20:7: "You shall not misuse the name of the LORD your God, for the LORD will not hold anyone guiltless who misuses his name." NIV.

"I am trying here to prevent anyone saying the really foolish thing that people often say about Him: I'm ready to accept Jesus as a great moral teacher, but I don't accept His claim to be God. That is the one thing we must not say. A man who was merely a man and said the sort of things that Jesus said would not be a great moral teacher. He would be a lunatic – on the level with the man who says he is a poached egg or else he would be the Devil of Hell. You must make your choice. Either this man was, and is, the Son of God, or else a madman or something worse. You can shut him up for a fool, you can spit at him and kill him as a demon or you can fall at his feet and call him Lord and God, but let us not come with any patronizing nonsense about his being a great human teacher. He has not left that open to us. He did not intend to."[53]

After the reports of Jesus's resurrection from the dead Thomas said,

Unless I see the nail marks in his hands and put my finger where the nails were, and put my hand into his side, I will not believe.[54]

Obviously, Thomas was one of those "seeing is believing" type of people. However, Jesus met with Thomas a week later and said to him,

---

[53] CS Lewis, *Mere Christianity*, 1952.
[54] John 20:25b NIV.

Put your finger here; see my hands. Reach out your hand and put it into my side. Stop doubting and believe.[55]

It was then that Thomas was changed from doubter into believer. For Thomas did not exclaim to Jesus, "Lunatic! Liar!" Rather "Thomas said to Him, 'My Lord and my God!' Then Jesus told him, 'Because you have seen me, you have believed; blessed are those who have not seen and yet have believed.'"[56]

If you hit your thumb while hammering in a nail, think of something other than yelling any of the LORD God's titles! Best just to say, "Ouch!" and leave it there. The rebellious Jews had the ruling Romans nail Jesus to the cross for blasphemy, for swearing, for allegedly taking the LORD God's name in vain, i.e., for supposedly breaking the Third Commandment. For Jesus was going around claiming to be God by making Himself equal to God.[57] Clearly they thought He was either a Liar or even a Lunatic. They did not believe that He was the Son of God.

One time as He was going around the place He sought His disciples' opinion as to who He was. This is where you can take a few moments to consider the opinions of plumbers, journalists and art teachers, butchers, bakers and candlestick makers. Who did your mum say Jesus was? Who did/does your dad, your teacher, your friends, your next door neighbour say Jesus is? Who did your local minister or priest or Atheist uncle say Jesus is?

---

[55] John 20:27 NIV.
[56] John 20:28-29 NIV.
[57] See e.g., Matthew 9:3; John 5:18.

When Jesus came to the region of Caesarea Philippi, he asked his disciples, 'Who do people say the Son of Man is?' They replied, 'Some say John the Baptist; others say Elijah; and still others, Jeremiah or one of the prophets.'[58]

This is where all your upbringing comes in, the movies you watched, the books and magazines you have read, the people in the pubs and clubs you have spoken to, the people you hung around with, your classmates at school. All of these and more influence us, our way of thinking. If Jesus really and truly is the Son of the living God then every last one of us would do well to come at the question of who Jesus is without all the background din, chatter and clatter of the busy school dining hall. Let there be silence! Away with everyone! It is hard to think clearly with the sound of a thousand different voices echoing in the temple of your mind. Silence! At this point I am reminded of the words to an old hymn,

God reveals His presence;
Let us now adore Him,
And with awe appear before Him.
God is in His temple;
All within keep silence...[59]

After hearing what His disciples said regarding who and what others claimed Jesus to be, He got personal and pointed the Sword of the Spirit at their hearts and jabbed. How are His disciples going to reply? Have they made up

[58] Matthew 16:13-14 NIV.
[59] Gerhard Tersteegen, 1697-1769, translated by Frederick William Foster, 1760-1835.

their minds as to who Jesus is because Bob the boatbuilder had an opinion? Or Ned the net-mender's pontifications? Or are they going to be like the Bereans and search the Scriptures to see if these things He claims about Himself are so? Anyway, Jesus didn't give His disciples any wiggle or wriggle room. You are either on His hook and safe on His boat or you're still lost at sea.

> 'But what about you? He asked. Who do you say I am?' Simon Peter answered, 'You are the Messiah, the Son of the living God.' Jesus replied, 'Blessed are you Simon son of Jonah, for this was not revealed to you by flesh and blood, but by my Father in heaven.'[60]

Only God can remove the scales from your eyes and reveal His Son to you. Yes, Jesus is the Son of God. But keep in mind that it's not you who gets to judge Him, but He who gets to judge you.

> Therefore since we are God's offspring, we should not think that the divine being is like gold or silver or stone—an image made by human design and skill. In the past God overlooked such ignorance, but now he commands all people everywhere to repent. For he has set a day when he will judge the world with justice by the man he has appointed. He has given proof of this to everyone by raising him from the dead.[61]

May He be gracious to you.

---

[60] Matthew 16:15-17 NIV.
[61] Acts 17:29-31 NIV.

A-mouldering in the Grave?

"John Brown's body lies a-mouldering in the grave" (repeated three times) and its chorus "Glory, glory, hallelujah" (also repeated three times) and followed with "His soul is marching on" is a well-known song. To be sure, multiple versions and variations arose as the song developed from the 1850s through the American Civil War. The tune apparently was an adaptation of the old song "Say, Brothers, Will You Meet Us," becoming "John Brown's Body" during the American Civil War, and then used for "The Battle Hymn of the Republic" (a.k.a. "Mine Eyes Have Seen the Glory"). At school we sang another version with the words of the chorus beginning with, "Glory, glory, hallelujah, the teacher hit me with a ruler..." And then there's the Union Workers' version, "Solidarity Forever".

The tune may be alive and well, but poor old John Brown's body lies a-mouldering in the grave. John Brown was an Abolitionist. Whereas John Brown sought to abolish slavery and was executed in its cause, Jesus Christ sought to abolish death and was executed in its cause! But only the body of one of these two lies a-mouldering in the grave. Can you guess which one? It's easy, isn't it? For we never sing about Jesus' body a-mouldering in the grave. Rather we sing things like,

> Jesus Christ is risen today, *Hallelujah!*
> Our triumphant holy day, *Hallelujah!*
> Who did once, upon the Cross, *Hallelujah!*
> Suffer to redeem our loss, *Hallelujah!*[62]

Or,

---

[62] Unknown author c. 1372 and translated by Lyra Davidica, 1708.

Up from the grave He arose,
With a mighty triumph o'er His foes,
He arose a victor from the dark domain.
And He lives forever, with His saints to reign.
He arose! He arose! Hallelujah! Christ arose![63]

The 17th century and brilliant theologian John Owen sums up what the resurrection of Jesus Christ means in the gripping title of one of his books, "The Death of Death in the Death of Christ." If the body of Jesus Christ still lies a-mouldering in the grave then, as the Apostle Paul poignantly puts it, "And if Christ has not been raised, your faith is futile; you are still in your sins."[64]

You could read books aplenty, they are legion, alleging that Jesus didn't really die on the cross, but only swooned and was resuscitated afterwards. And others claiming that His bones really do lie a-mouldering in a grave in Palestine, though they're not exactly sure where or which one. The bottom line is that only God can convince you of the reality of Christ's physical resurrection from the dead.[65] Only the Spirit working with the Word can convict you into believing that the Son of God rose bodily from the tomb. However, you should know that to deny this is to call God a liar! And, as the Apostle Paul went on to say, "If only for this life we have hope in Christ, we are of all people most to be pitied."[66]

The literal rising of Jesus Christ from the realm of the dead is the very heart and soul of Christianity. No resurrection, no Christianity! It means that the One who

---

[63] Robert Lowry, 1826-99.
[64] 1 Corinthians 15:17 (NIV).
[65] See e.g., Mark 12:18.
[66] 1 Corinthians 15:19 (NIV).

said, "Destroy this temple and I will raise it again in three days"[67] is a liar or a lunatic or both! If Jesus has not been resurrected then neither will you or I be resurrected. This means that we do not and cannot have everlasting or eternal life, as the Bible promises we have by grace through faith in Jesus Christ.

Do you remember what Jesus, just before He went to the cross, said to Peter and the other disciples?

> You will all fall away. For it is written: 'I will strike the shepherd, and the sheep will be scattered.' But after I have risen, I will go ahead of you into Galilee. Peter declared, 'Even if all fall away, I will not.' 'Truly I tell you,' Jesus answered, 'today – yes, tonight before the rooster crows twice you yourself will disown me three times.' But Peter insisted emphatically, 'Even if I have to die with you, I will never disown you.' And all the others said the same.[68]

Some of the saddest times for Christians is whenever they think and feel that they have somehow let their Lord down by not standing up for Him and identifying with Him whenever they were given opportunity. Peter went further than that. Some servant girls had spotted Peter when Jesus' arrest was going on. They knew that he was one of Jesus' disciples. But three times he kept on denying it whenever they saw him and accused him of such.

> After a little while, those standing near said to Peter, 'Surely you are one of them, for you are a Galilean.' He began to call down curses, and he swore to them,

---

[67] John 2:19 (NIV).
[68] Mark 14:27-31.

'I don't know this man you're talking about.' Immediately the rooster crowed the second time. Then Peter remembered the word Jesus had spoken to him; 'Before the rooster crows twice you will disown me three times.' And he broke down and wept.[69]

However, Peter and the rest of the disciples were soon transformed from being so weak and feeble into something strong and bold after Jesus had arisen from the dead. They went from being the cowardly cowering to becoming the emboldened empowered. If the body of Jesus lay a-mouldering in the grave then this dramatic about-face change that came over the disciples would be inexplicable. Subsequently, Peter, filled and fortified by the Holy Spirit stood before the "Men of Israel" and preached the Gospel, the Good News of Jesus Christ to them. In his sermon he didn't mention anything about Jesus a-mouldering in the grave, but rather the opposite, stating among other things,

> Fellow Israelites, I can tell you confidently that the patriarch David died and was buried, and his tomb is here to this day. But he was a prophet and knew that God had promised him on oath that he would place one of his descendants on his throne. Seeing what was to come, he spoke of the resurrection of the Messiah, that he was not abandoned to the realm of the dead, nor did his body see decay. God has raised this Jesus to life, and we are all witnesses to it. Exalted to the right hand of God, he has received

---

[69] Mark 14:70-72 (NIV).

from the Father the promised Holy Spirit and has poured out what you now see and hear.[70]

As I conclude this it is my hope and prayer that you have understood the essential claims of Jesus that we have covered in this short work, that you really and actually have encountered the risen Jesus Christ, and that He has transformed and has emboldened you by pouring out on you and thereby filling you also with His Spirit, just as He did Peter and His other disciples after His resurrection from the grave and ascension into heaven.

---

[70] Acts 2:29-33 (NIV).

The one to whom this book is dedicated is the same one who challenged me to write it. He is the one who said, "Try to convince the reader why he should believe that Jesus is the Son of God." I hope this simple book goes a long way to helping to convince you that Jesus IS the Son of God. Let me close with my friend's words from a recent email to me:

> Neil,
> I carry upon my person A4 sheets on which I have written –
> "LIFE... not Death."
> "The Resurrection is not just a Bible story. It was an actual historical event. The evidence of the New Testament is dependable and compelling. Jesus was as dead as a Roman execution could make him, then he was demonstrably alive. To the many witnesses of the risen Christ it was not a matter of faith but a matter of factual personal experience, so real and so tremendous that they were prepared to come out of hiding and, at risk to their lives, proclaim it to the world."
> "Jesus Christ actually rose from the dead – Doesn't that make you think?"
> I place these sheets in bus shelters, supermarket trolleys, pub doorways... anywhere they may be found and hopefully read. Like the Parable of the Sower, if I may make such a comparison.
> sincerely,
> Billy

CPSIA information can be obtained
at www.ICGtesting.com
Printed in the USA
BVHW031403210519
548914BV00001B/10/P